Exploring the Heartland

An Agenda for the Media

Editor
Umashanker Phadnis

GYAN PUBLISHING HOUSE
New Delhi - 110002

in collaboration with
Press Institute of India
New Delhi

EXPLORING THE HEARTLAND
An Agenda for the Media
(Media)

ISBN : 81-212-0595-6

Published in 1998 in India by
Gyan Publishing House
5, Ansari Road
New Delhi 110 002
Laser Typesetting : Grow Computers, Delhi.
Printed at Mehra Offset Press, New Delhi

Contents

Preface 7

1. Myth and Reality 9
2. Fact and Fiction 17
3. Crisis to Chaos 29
4. A Challenge Met 41
5. Trends in the Hindi Press 51

Preface

This publication is a succinct account of the proceedings of three workshops organised by the Press Institute to promote the coverage of human development problems of which not much notice has been taken by the media, particularly the press. The workshops had been designed to enable media persons to interact with field activists, both non-official and official, in human development services to ensure wider and more constructive coverage.

Those who participated in these exercises were senior media news managers of the rank of news editors and special correspondents, officials handling human development affairs at the policy making levels of the administration and a number of field activists belonging to non-official organisations. Thus, the entire gamut of persons involved in the promotion of human development had been brought together for discussing a common agenda.

The outline of the discussions which took place in these exercises sketched here deals with the scope for mediapersons to cover the grassroot reality, whether as news items, feature articles or investigative reportage. The need for this being disseminated is widely emphasised by the depressingly low status in India of the various indices of the quality of human life brought out in the reports of the UNDP with unfailing regularity year after year.

A senior administrator has held out the warning of a situation of "low intensity civil conflict" prevailing in the Hindi speaking areas of the country that would degenerate further if the present trend is not arrested and reversed.

Various aspects of this impending but avoidable pessimistic social prognosis emerge out of the observations contained in this publication. These will, hopefully, induce a measure of urgency on the part of the media to act as a catalytic agent of change in the prevailing indifferent attitude towards vital issues of human development.

Ajit Bhattacharjea
(Director, Press Institute of India)

1

Myth and Reality

Umashanker Phadnis

For some time now, media monitors have been noting with disquiet the predominantly elitist orientation of the Indian press and its increasing alienation from the basic concerns of the general mass of its readership community. Arguably, such a growth pattern of the press may well be attributed to the nature of socio-economic development which had taken place in the last couple of decades. Media managers, however, have to ponder over the broader consequences of this warped and skewed outlook on the part of the media on society and its integrity, in general, and the political system and its viability, in particular.

A distressing aspect of this media situation is the distortion in the media-reader relationship which has surfaced in a pronounced manner in the Hindi press serving the country's heartland states of Bihar, Uttar Pradesh, Madhya Pradesh, Rajasthan, Haryana and Himachal Pradesh. Accounting for a total population of some 350 million, a highly disconcerting characteristic of this region is the socio-economic profile of this population which has been compared to some of the worst regions of the world in terms of the quality of life indices. Such is the neglect on the part of the media on this state of affairs in its backyard, its readership area, that it has yet to ask itself why such a situation has developed and whether at all it has a role in mitigating it and arresting its further spread.

The virtual abandonment of its obligation and responsibility to mirror the reality of the socio-economic milieu has wider implications. Basically, it is a blatant violation of the professional ethics of mediapersons to be objective and truthful to its readership community. Furthermore, this neglect tends to generate a sense of complacency in a harmonious society which, on the contrary, is beset with conflicts and contradictions.

The consequences of portraying an unreal and distorted scenario on the political system has been brought out in bold relief in the case of the erstwhile Soviet Union or Yugoslavia. Or, for that matter, in India itself when it had a brief brush with the experience of living with a controlled or a muffled press during the emergency.

To be sure, the Hindi Press is not operating in such a political environment but there is no evidence either of its being aware of its responsibility to stem a further deterioration in the universally acceptable norms of a civil society.

Pegged on this assessment of this dilemma of the media by a number of leading media persons in the Hindi press, the Press Institute has launched on a series of exercises dealing with a number of inadequacies with which the media is beset. These were a flawed portrayal of society in which the life styles of the rich and the powerful tended to push out of focus the privations of the poor and the meek. Nor did the media project or interpret constructively the struggles waged by the deprived and dispossessed sections of the population. Finally, there is not much evidence of its fulfilling of the responsibility resting on it to secure the right of the people for a dignified life as a primacy in national priorities so that it emerges as a compulsive factor in political culture.

In this context, to enable the Hindi press evolve a perspective which it needs to, and can, play in the emerging situation, the Press Institute had called a conference of Hindi editors last August to work out a programme of action to reorient the press to meet the demands on it. The conference unanimously formulated a series of steps which the Press Institute could take to induce Hindi mediapersons bring the newspapers closer to its readership community.

In his keynote address at the meeting, poverty economist Lakshmi Jain focussed his presentation on the consequences of superimposing an economic regime geared to a criteria of conspicuous consumption on a society where an overwhelming majority of population live below the poverty line or barely manage to subsist on its borderline. Interlacing economic data with visual evidence of the deplorably indigent conditions of the living conditions of this section, Jain highlighted the inevitable consequence of the prevailing pattern of economy in accentuating pressures for the further impoverishment of the poor.

A basic issue confronting the Hindi press in projecting this scenario which Prabash Joshi pinpointed at the conference was the value premise conditioning the media in respect of newsworthiness and its social commitment. He emphasised that as a result the media was inclined to consider the wants of a few were more important than the needs of the many. He decried the tendency on the part of the Hindi press to adopt unquestioningly hackneyed stereotypes serving as models of English newspapers both in range and priorities of news coverage and its presentation. He warned the editors that if they persisted with this approach, it would result in distancing the newspapers even further from the community of its readers. In those circumstances, he called upon the editors to adopt an innovative approach so that Hindi newspapers could acquire an identity of their own, articulating the concerns of the population.

In the ensuing discussion, the meeting was unanimous in its opinion that the view expressed by Prabash Joshi should be widely discussed at all levels especially among those involved in the production of newspapers such as reporters and desk managers. Specifically, the meeting suggested as a first step a workshop of news editors and senior correspondents whose co-operation would be vital in providing the newspapers with a new orientation. The meeting was also of the view that this required to be followed by appropriate meetings down the line to the level of district and field level reporters so that there is an identity of purpose among all those engaged in the production of the newspaper.

It was also of the view that the programme of re-orientation should highlight investigative techniques into different aspects of rural life. Moreover, the participants pointed out that media persons required to imbibe the art of putting across their ideas in a manner that their reports brought out the human dimension of the cold statistical data available to them. Or, as Ajit Bhattacharjea pointed out in his opening remarks at the Bhopal workshop: "To make any feature story about rural India come alive, to cover a process of social change requires a different kind of writing. It is a great challenge. Sometimes it is like literature. If it is properly handled, it is the nearest thing to literature."

To give effect to the suggestions made at the meeting was a three-day workshop held last September in Bhopal. Its format was so planned that it provided an opportunity for senior news managers, namely, of the level of special correspondents and news editors to interact not only with each other but also with administrators, representatives of non-governmental organisations and field activists.

The agenda of the workshop covered the entire gamut of problems relating to rural life, such as the working of the panchayati raj system of governance, its role in poverty alleviation or its elimination. Government sponsored schemes of development and anti-poverty programmes, living conditions of the tribals and other deprived sections of society came under scrutiny.

In stimulating the discussions on the theme of changes and their repercussions for better or worse on different sections of population in the rural areas, P Sainath. the noted authority on rural poverty and author of the well known book *Everybody Loves a Good Drought,* portrayed in real life terms, the impact of some of the government's programmes ostensibly intended for people's "welfare". Providing a clue for investigating reporters of these schemes, he described in detail the methodology of delving into below-the-surface reality through the means of statistical data and empirical observation. The approach enunciated by Sainath was that correspondents should not regard a particular development as an episode in itself but examine it in the context of being the end product of a process, often involving clash of sectoral interests among various groups of people.

In an extraordinarily frank and forthright exposition, the principal secretary of the Madhya Pradesh government in charge of education, Sudeep Banerjee, portrayed a grim scenario of the conditions of life of tribal communities and the unabated exploitation to which they were subjected. He had no hesitation in describing the situation in vast tracts of rural Madhya Pradesh, particularly in the districts predominantly inhabited by the tribals and scheduled castes as no different as far as living conditions were concerned from the poverty ridden populations of sub-Saharan states of Africa. Banerjee was emphatic in his assessment that in the circumstances prevailing in Madhya Pradesh there was a situation of low-intensity civil conflict in which the state seemed to have the upper hand.

In contrast to the situation in these African states, Banerjee spotted a redeeming factor on the Indian scenario. This was that the prevailing system provided political space enough for the dispossessed to struggle for their rights whereas such was not the case in the sub-Saharan states which drifted from one authoritarian rule to another without any relevance to people's interests. He expected the media to play a constructive role in mobilising the political strength of the downtrodden.

Banerjee, however, deplored the tendency of the media as well as the administration to wish away the tension - ridden environment of the areas inhabited by the tribals and the scheduled castes not only in Madhya Pradesh but also in the other states of the Hindi - speaking regions. He warned: "If we are not alert in the next few years, our social and political conditions would deteriorate to the type of situation in sub-Saharan Africa though for the time being there seems to be scope enough for improvements which can be brought about in reconciling conflicts and contradictions with which the society in this region is beset."

Referring to the low level of literacy in the Hindi speaking region Banerjee pointed out the dismal situation in which the proportion of illiterates in the Hindi-speaking population equalled that of the illiterates in all the other languages put together. In the course of the discussion, many other participants came out with suggestions for bolstering literacy levels of the population if the media was to become an effective instrument of change. A common thread running through the suggestions they put forward for the promotion of literacy was that for this movement to succeed it should be related to their day-to-day problems.

On the issue of the media and the administration, S C Behar, adviser to the Madhya Pradesh Chief Minister, made no attempt to gloss over the shortcomings of the government and provided an insight into the various pressures and pulls operating on the administration which vitiated good governance. At the same time, he did not hesitate to question the manner in which newspapers conducted themselves. He saw there was a great deal of validity in the allegation of an NGO participant who felt that often the man in the street was at a loss to know whether he should trust the authorities or the press.

Drawing upon his personal experience as an administrator at various levels, Behar attributed the lackadaisical approach to the responsibilities with which administrators were saddled to the lack of an alert media providing correctives.

As intended, the thrust of the discussions at the workshop was on keeping mediapersons acquainted with the grassroot reality from different points of view. Another purpose was to foster a measure of rapport among the participants in their respective roles. While there was a great deal of constructive heart-searching in this respect, there was also a measure of despondency that there had been little or no impact at the macro level in bringing about a qualitative change in attitudes to usher in purposeful goals in governance.

That this consideration, which ought to be the overriding factor influencing political objectives, was conspicuously absent in the recent poll campaign was brought out in a news analysis conducted by the Press Institute. Commenting on this situation, Ajit Bhattacharjea noted, "This is a sad reflection on the media as well as the NGOs. They have failed to create adequate public awareness of the national importance of the issues" relating to people's welfare.

Included here are two contrasting experiences in NGO-media interface recalled at the conference, one bringing out the salutary impact of a well coordinated effort between the NGO and the media and the other, of the failure to evolve rapport between the two.

There was, for instance, the happy experience of S R Hiremath of the Samaj Parivartan Samudaya in its interface with the press in activities related to integrated rural development in Karnataka. In the course of its activities, the Samudaya came up with a formidable confrontation with a joint project involving the Birlas in respect of a joint project poly-fibre mill being set up in North Karnataka. The project involved several thousand villagers being dispossessed of their land so that an eucalyptus farm could be set up to provide raw material for the plant.

After a relentless struggle, the Samudaya eventually succeeded in securing abandonment of the project. Recalling his experience of this struggle, Hiremath noted, "Generally speaking we have had a very good experience with the media. But having said that, I would also like to emphasise that unless you have comprehensive media coverage, the issues do not go very far."

On the contrary was the experience of Bharat Dogra who, besides being a field activist in developmental activities was also a freelance journalist. He had no hesitation in his assessment: "Our newspapers on the one hand promote consumerism fully and on the other say two or three nice things about environment protection. I think there is a lot of hypocrisy in this. Those who are genuinely interested in the media playing a relevant role in telling people what environment protection means and development ought to be have a lot of hard thinking to do."

Finally, there was an indepth review of the present state of Hindi newspapers and in the discussions, the participants highlighted the pressures under which the field reporters function. A number of remedial measures were forthcoming to enable the newspapers to reflect the ground situation more extensively and in depth than they are able to do at present.

This brief review of the proceedings of the three workshops organised by the Press Institute will, hopefully, stimulate further interest and thought among media persons on how the press could respond constructively to the social tensions prevailing in the heartlands in an acute form but are endemic in other regions.

The presentations made at these workshops have identified the precise nature of the pressures and pulls operating on which the rural society, particularly its defenceless segments. This was the running theme of the workshops conceived to help the media discover new roots in a society in the flux of superimposed change. Some of the proceedings were in Hindi. They have been translated and edited by **Punam Thakur** of *The Pioneer*. The main presentations follow.

2
Fact and Fiction

P. Sainath
Author of ***'Everybody Love A God Drought'*** *and several other well-known books on rural poverty in India*

Let me preface my presentation with my firm belief that there is enormous talent among rural journalists in India. Since 1973, I have been travelling all over India and have visited Tamil Nadu, Kerala, Andhra Pradesh, Madhya Pradesh, Bihar and Orissa. I have come across very rich talent in these states.

One of the finest journalists I have come across is based in Kalahandi, less than 170 kms. from Raipur. This 25-year-old man, Purshottam Singh Thakur, started the *Jan Madhyam,* a newspaper. The paper reached a circulation of 3,000 copies in one year without any advertising support. The Collector of Nawapada closed it down because it had called the Collector corrupt. The Collector was then transferred on those charges. The Press Council has been sitting on the case for one-and-a-half years. But what is astonishing is that all the charges made by Purshottan Singh Thakur about hunger related deaths in Kalahandi have been upheld by the National Human Rights Commission and by the Commission of the Orissa Assembly. They have also been discussed in Parliament and the Parliament has been told that the charges have been confirmed.

Here is one young man, 25 years old and the rest of us are not able to do anything for the paper that has been closed down for airing the truth. I have personally read that story. I even went to that area. The story is hundred per cent correct. And the Human Rights Commission has itself upheld the decision. They are not able to come to the rescue of this young person. But something is being done. Something positive is happening now. I can tell you that much.

Today when I was listening to your experiences in the morning, they are all so true, because I hear the same experience in Pudukkottai in Tamil Nadu and I hear the same experience in Bilaspur in Madhya Pradesh. People are experiencing many common problems.

The second point that I want to make is that the future of print media in India is very bright. This is one country in the world where the rise in literacy rates is yet to cover millions of people. When literacy spreads what the position will be is a different question. But if you take the case of Kerala, you will not find such a high saturation of papers per population anywhere on the planet. It is very rare. There are papers with circulations of seven lakhs, five lakhs, four lakhs and magazines with a circulation of three lakhs in Kerala. That is what literacy has done. So if we improve literacy standards in this country, the print media has quite a tremendous future. I am very optimistic.

Having told you what I am optimistic about now let me tell you what I am sorry for. I do not think that rural reporting is going to take place in the preseant framework of crisis reporting.

I will explain what I mean. We complain about Western media. If you read *New York Times, Washington Post* or *London Times*, you will see that India is a place of famine, poverty, death, earthquakes. We are all angry about that. But we do exactly the same thing to our rural areas. We report on rural areas when there is a plague, when there is unnatural death, when there is a disaster. But we have to stop looking at crisis as an event and start looking at crisis as a process.

If 200 people have died in the Palamu district of Bihar in shooting in the last two months, it is an event. But there was a process behind this event. There was a deteriorating situation which we have not reported. We have to report that process. We have to report the daily life of people and what is happening to it. For that we have to know who the people are, who the poor are in India. Forty per cent of the Indian poor are landless agricultural labourers. And 45 per cent of the Indian poor are small or very marginal labourers. Eightyfive per cent of India's poor people have no land — not even one acre. This is the first important thing that we should know if we are to cover our rural areas. Who are we looking at? I think this is important for several reasons.

I made an analysis of big newspapers in Bombay, Delhi and other cities. I tried to find out what the beats of the full time correspondents were. The largest number of correspondents are political correspondents. The new tribes that are emerging in large numbers are business correspondents. There are 11 correspondents engaged in business beats in a non-financial daily. According to my calculations, less than two per cent of the population has any shares. But you have 11 reporters covering the markets.

Look within. What are our priorities? Eightyfive per cent of the population is landless labourers, or small or marginal farmers. How many correspondents are covering them? Instead we also have a third tribe of sports correspondents. They are the biggest tribe. There are also cricket correspondents. Some big newspapers also have full time golf correspondents. They cover only golf all through the year. Then metro papers have beats. There are ministry correspondents and specialised correspondents like defence and cultural correspondents. In Bombay we also have fashion correspondents, glamour correspondents, eating out correspondents. You can find glamour correspondents and eating out correspondents, but can you find even one full time correspondent for the rural poor? Even for education we do not have more than two or three full time correspondents in the country. And when I say education I mean college campus in the national press. Not primary schools. This is a country where 70 to 100 million children are outside the school system. One in every third child labourer in the world is in India. One in every four children outside the school system in the world is in India. But we do not have anyone covering this on a full time basis. Covering this is considered a waste of talent and a waste of funds.

There are methods even within the existing base, within the existing situation for dealing with this. Rural reporting is not only about gathering news on how many wells have been dug, how many roads have been laid and how many tanks have been constructed. If you look at it from the lives of ordinary people, the sinking of a bore well is an important and dramatic event. I will give you an example of what happened in Pudukkottai in Tamil Nadu. Very often we go to the village when the minister goes there. The mantri goes, cuts the ribbon and inaugurates a school building. We all go with him. And we return with him. But no one looks at what happens later. My point is that regular reporting is more important than special reporting. Regular, deep reporting is more important. Covering an area more regularly so that you get more experience. Then when there is a major crisis, you can do justice to that area.

There was a famine in Kovilpatti village in Pudukkottai district of south Tamil Nadu. The press wrote extensively about it and the government went on the defensive and ordered the sinking of 2,000 bore wells in the area. What happened after they were sunk? The event was welcomed with great fanfare in the press which even took credit for getting the wells sunk.

But this is where the problems started. Nobody raised the question that if 2,000 wells were sunk here what will happen to the ground water table? Secondly, nobody asked on whose lands the wells were being sunk. In Kovilpatti I was witness to a spectacular situation after the wells were sunk. There are two communities the Muthurajas (Harijans), OBC, MBC, and the Reddiar community which is the forward caste. The Reddiar community has political clout so 25 wells were sunk on their farms. There was so much of drama because of the sinking of these wells that it started five processes.

Firstly, all the traditionally sunk wells in the Muthuraja areas dried up because the bore wells in the Reddiar areas were sunk much deeper. This led to another problem: Since it was the farming season the Muthurajas started approaching the Reddiars for water. This started the second process. The Reddiars started selling water. Such emergence of private water markets is starting in all parts of India where there is famine. This is not restricted to Tamil Nadu alone.

This started the third process because in this village the good land is with Muthurajas as the Reddiars migrated here from Andhra Pradesh some one hundred years ago. Hence the Reddiars do not have good land. The good land is with the Muthurajas. Since he is selling him water his production becomes uneconomical and he spends more money on agriculture than he was spending earlier. If he wanted water for 30 days, what the Reddiar did was to give him water for 22-25 days and then close it. Now he wants water for five more days. Then a Muthuraja comes to him and the Reddiar gives him. But to give him water he demands everything else he needs, but not water. Now the Reddiar tells him, in that case you must give me 1/5th of your crop. So the Muthiraja has taken the money and now the Reddiar takes the crop from him. Now this is the rate in southern Tamil Nadu: one-fifth of the crop. That is the third process.

The fourth process is that he gets into debt. Because his produce becomes uneconomical, one-fifth of the crop he has to give to the Reddiar. He has paid for water. On top of it he is in debt. If he is in debt from whom will he take money? From the Reddiar. This is the fourth process.

The fifth process: he is unable to pay the debt. The Reddiar takes his land. In one small village in the past 8-10 years, 70 acres have changed hands from the poor community to the rich community in a small village. These days all Muthurajas are landless. Therefore they become landless labourers. One technique is to go with the minister, cut ribbons and then announce that the minister has given bore wells. What are the consequences of this development for the ordinary people? Let me take an example from Kalahandi in Orissa, far away from Pudukottai.

The second example I have already spoken about. I have taken the name of Thakur. For eight to ten months, Kalahandi was in crisis. Many eminent journalists arrived on the scene although they could not even point out Kalahandi on the map. The Collector lectured to them that there had been an 80 per cent successful rabi crop. Rural journalists did not buy that nonsense. The big reporters from cities bought that nonsense. They were all taking notes. I was sitting next to the window, the Collector was saying that "we had performed experiments in our laboratories. Our experiments say that rabi crop is going to be 80 per cent successful."

However, outside the collectorate in the fields, farmers are letting their cattle eat the crop! Because the crop has failed so miserably, they were saying that at least whatever is available, let the cattle eat it. Because the cattle were dying. So they were letting them eat what little was left of the rabi crop. Did you listen to the Collector or did you use your eyes to look outside the collectorate and see why the people were allowing the cattle to eat their crops since the crops had failed.

There are many such simple techniques to question the authenticity of official claims. I can tell you about source techniques as well. The source material that I use is the same as all of you might be using. There was a big debate about hunger deaths. Were there deaths or not? The second debate was about migration to Raipur, Madhya Pradesh from Kalahandi. This was a great debate in the Orissa Assembly. One claim was that migration doubled. The Collector, Nawapada, Madhya Pradesh, and the district administration claimed that there was not much of a migration. May be a little, not much. What do the reporters do then?

They take the version of the Collector. The Collector says that migration has not increased. They go to the NGO. NGO people say that migration has increased. Now it is balanced. They report that the Collector says this and the NGO says this and confuse the reader as to what is the truth. They could have adopted some small techniques. To get to the bottom of the story all they had to do was to go to the bus station and ask the supervisor of the bus station, "Gentleman, how many buses ply from here to Raipur everyday?" He said daily 11 buses ply. Eleven buses from one town of Kalahandi to Raipur. I asked how many direct buses from Raipur to Kalahandi? He said three. Because others are going via different routes. But from Kalahandi there are three buses. Last year, this time, how many buses were there from Kalahandi-Raipur. He answered that there were four. Four has turned to eleven. That meant that migration has more than doubled.

Then we went to the railway station and asked the station superintendent how many tickets have been sold to Raipur. He said, "Sir, we ran out of card paper. We are issuing tickets on plain paper." This goes to show how much migration has increased. Thus there are many little techniques that we can use without being dependent on the government. These techniques are open to us.

We should say that the government says that migration has come down or they have become static. But you should also add that on the basis of the information I gathered from the bus and rail stations, migration has increased manifold. Then the reader gets the message as to what is the truth. That this is authentic. And it is not the cooked up version of some government official. The bus station superintendent is also an official source for the transport department. The railway station superintendent is also an official source. When you show the contradiction between the official and your own sources you get a story.

By suppressing the truth the person who is suffering will suffer even more because his problem has not been highlighted. There is even less chance of something happening. When Purushottam Thakur wrote the story about the hunger related death, and the Collector denied it, and the administration denied this and closed his newspaper. Because he highlighted the problem it came up in the Assembly. There was a chance of solution. I do not see myself as a messiah providing solution. My job is of a journalist. I am a reporter. I am not providing the solution.

Q: Sometimes we find it in the larger interest to suppress news. I am a reporter from Punjab and during the communal riots there, true information tended to be inflammatory which was not in the wider interests of society.

A: I understand your point. I will respond to the question you are raising. It might apply in certain ethical situations, say when there is a communal riot. Then you must use your discretion. I have covered most of the communal riots since Meerut, 1982 till January, 1993. There have been many situations where I have not necessarily written everything that I know. Because I do not want my freedom to cost someone else his life in the next round of riots when the government is unable to protect the lives of people. So I agree with you on that.

Coming to Madhya Pradesh, I think there are a thousand stories in every village. Second thing, this is one state which made an attempt in creating some kind of a database in the form of Human Development Report. When you look at the MP Human Development Report, it tells you the percentage of people using the primary health centre at Sargujah as 0.93 per cent. You have a story right in that figure. If less than one person in a hundred is using health services, I want to go to the primary health centre and find out why. My technique is very simple. I am a loafer. I will go and hang around in a village for 5-6 days. You sit in a village for five days. You will get ten stories.

Land, water and forests. These are the biggest issues. But the issue for me is the rights. What are the rights of the Indian people. assured to them by the Constitutional Fundamental Rights and in the Directive Principles of State Policy. We have to write about that daily. Then we can look for solutions. Constant reiterations of these facts are necessary because in this country justice and law are so arbitrary. For instance, a man is taken out of jail under police custody in Khargaon, murdered by a mob after he is taken out of the safety of the jail. I cannot believe it. So in the interest of national security do we keep quiet about Khargaon?

I feel that a reporter must be assigned two or three districts which he must visit regularly, and he knows these districts, becomes familiar with these districts. For me the first thing that the reporter should know is the agriculture of the district. If he does not know the agriculture of a rural district, you do not know the district.

Secondly, read the Gazetteer. Bastar's Gazetteer does not exist and Chattisgarh's Gazetteer has been withdrawn because it carried a controversial story of a religious movement. However, many other districts have fairly good Gazetteers. There is a tremendous source of information in a Gazetteer on the history, politics and culture of the region. I think this is the minimum in this country for a reporter to do. He must read the district Gazetteer.

Thirdly, he must see detailed census abstracts of the districts which he is going to cover. Fourthly, he must consult the material available in the common libraries in the city that is the Centre for Monitoring Indian Economies, District Profiles, CMI District Profile.

There is one more source. Probationer IAS officers when they come to a district they are given an assignment to write about the district. I find that some of the reports filed by these probationers are very good. Then they are still very young and very enthusiastic. Full of idealism that is still at work. So some of these probationers' reports on the district are very good. Because that person has access. He is able to get the information.

I will give you one more example. Simply by hanging out, simply by being a loafer and hanging out at a field point, you can get some stories. I will now narrate an incident. I will not reveal the name. It will be total contempt of court. When I say rights of people, I think one of the very important things is to look at what is access of the ordinary Indians to the justice system of this country? I visited the lowest unit of the court, Sub-Divisional Magistrate (SDM) of one district in Bihar. I was there for three days. From those three days I had material enough for twenty-five stories. What is it to be an adivasi? What is it to be a Harijan? What is it to be a poor Indian? And go to the court seeking justice?

First thing that happens in a court is that the advocate abuses the client because he is of the lower caste. The advocate discriminates against him at that point. He will even betray his clients' interests. This is number one.

The second thing is the harassment by the court clerk for bribe. There he has to give money. And I saw an extraordinary Magistrate. In spite of many years of court reporting, I have never seen a Magistrate like that. He is an SDM. It is not even a Sessions Court or High Court. You won't believe it but in two-and-a-half-hours he passed thirty-six bail applications on crimes like murder, rape, firing on police party! A man who confesses on firing on a police party gets a bail for Rs. 4,000 This SDM gives you bail for crimes in which even the High Court cannot give you bail.

The second story is of successful bail applications which were moved by one advocate who was related to the Magistrate. Since the other lawyers were rendered without business, therefore, when they knew that I was a journalist, they gheraoed me saying, look this is what is happening here. The 36 bail applications which were processed by this relative lawyer of the presiding SDM, on every bail application, money changed hands. On each and every bail application, money changed hands. And then negotiations were going on between different parties.

A corrupt Block Development Officer (BDO) came. And what he said you cannot hear that even in a Bollywood film. He was asking for bribes from a few young people. He takes 25 per cent. If the work to be done in your village costs Rs. 10,000, then he should be given Rs. 2,500. This is the rate, it has to be given. He went to one village, Eshak village, a communist village. There was a young boy. He became emotional, it was the question of his pride, self-respect. Next day they came to the BDO's office and called him out. He had demanded 25 per cent, isn't it? Twentyfive young men came there and beat him 25 times with their chappals. Then the BDO filed a case of dacoity, brigandry, murder, etc., against these boys. When the case was in the process, I was there. The BDO was telling them, "I am willing to drop the cases, I bear you no grudge", he is a businessmen. He was telling the leader of the group, "*are yaar, sir ko mara, dil ko mara, izzat ko mara arre hai pet me math maro*, give me my 25 per cent, I will do your work and withdraw my case against you, I have got my transfer already." These kind of negotiations were going on in the court right in front of everybody.

Just by going to these places and spending some time there are hundreds of stories like this to be gathered. But this needs the reporter to have basic knowledge of administration, basic understanding of district law and order. That education has to be given.

Seventeen years ago when I started in this profession, we had one basic motto: check it out. I went to Kharguja district to village Rajketa. Now we all know that any project in rural Madhya Pradesh is started in the name of adivasis because there is a lot of money here. In village Rajketa too a road was being laid in the name of Pahari Karuas at a cost of Rs. 18 lakh. A board had been put up saying that this road was meant for Pahari Karuas, the breakup of Rs. 17.44 lakh was also given. Now if we had probed a bit we would have found out that this is not a Pahari Karua village, it is a Gond village and there is only one Pahari Karua who lives three kilometres away from the road. Even the road was not a metalled one, though it had to be 6 metres only 4 and a half metres of kuccha road had been made.

There is another important point which needs to be highlighted. If a reporter knows the basic facts of the district he is covering, if he reads the abstracts of census data with him, he will know whether this is Gond village, whether it is a Pahari village, you can get this in the detailed abstracts. You have the Human Development Report, data base, I think all of you should demand that this data be made available to you on line in the press centres here or in any of the major cities.

This data is already in computer point. The Human Development Report data is in the computer point. Why should the press centres in Bhopal, Indore, Gwalior, not have access to these data on line? There has been value added to the data. It has been updated. I think you all should demand the government gives you access to the text. The quality of the report is not consistent. But some of the chapters are really good. Dealing with a country of 950 million people we need some gross data, some broad indicators. On the basis of this you can write the story of an individual. Even if you are choosing to write about an individual, you should find out whether he is representative of that village. Is he the representative of a particular community. If you have a broad data picture of the community you will know whether the person you have chosen is representative or not. Even when you write about an individual you are looking at the community through him.

I feel that we need two kinds of education for a reporter: The first is a course in individual human rights and the constitutional rights of an Indian. What are the fundamental rights and Directive Principles of State Policy.

If I am right then in 1993 the Supreme Court ruled that education is a justiciable right, and thus moved it into the realm of fundamental rights. So why are we talking about throwing crumbs at people? When children in Madhya Pradesh have a right to education, why are they not getting it? This is what I call a crisis because there is a violation of fundamental rights. Why don't we take it up from that angle? That a human right, a fundamental right of a young citizen of India is being violated by the state. I think there are a number of issues which we can discuss if we work within this framework:

(a) The reporting process.

(b) Looking at the daily lives of ordinary people.

(c) Link the ordinary people or the individual as a pick of a community or society as a whole.

(d) Try drawing a broad picture of what is happening in the processes of change, in the process of backwardness.

(e) To move out of the framework of crisis reporting and making rural India a part of our daily coverage.

Dr. Rajan Katoch

Secretary, Institutional Finance, Government of Madhya Pradesh

I want to talk to you about the human resource development reports, Manav Vikas Prativedhan, which the government has been compiling for public awareness since 1995 in Madhya Pradesh. I will confine myself to the Prativedhan and not about human resource development which is a very vast subject.

This law, which was made in 1995, aimed at focussing attention on subjects of illiteracy, health and livelihood. These issues can be understood in two or three segments. The importance of human resources can be understood in various contexts. The economic conditions have improved in various places though the standard of living has not improved. The rich have become richer and the poor are uneducated and their level of illiteracy is still lower. So economic development is not enough till it is complemented with health, literacy and means of livelihood. This was the main aim of the Prativedhan.

Why MP? Because it is believed that MP is a part of the four states which are called 'bimaru' states. And at distinctive characterstic of these states is the low levels of quality of life indicators. For instance, barring Himachal Pradesh, literacy levels are among the lowest in the country. Under the circumstances, it was felt that if would helpful to policy-makers if they could have at their disposal human development data periodically collated. Incidentally, MP was the first state to bring out this data.

What I would like to say about the report is that though it has been a brought out by the administration it is an independent one. We had formed a special consultative committee for this and the contents of the report have not been edited to give a slant to the views expressed in it. Basically, the effort was to use the UNDP yardsticks in MP and to see how they work here. Along with this we have shown the situation as far as literacy, health and means of livelihood are concerned. The report has therefore, statistics compiled by experts. All this is based on secondary data. No new surveys were done. The ideal situation would be to do this survey but the state is so vast that this would have taken years. So we have tried to get a snapshot vision and we can collect all the information that is available at present.

What we feel is that this has made an impact in the last one and a half to two years. Whenever we talk of human resources these issues are in the limelight and there has been some pressure on the administration as well. We can show the administration that this is the situation and ask it what it has done to improve it. There is potential for this to be an action document. Whether something concrete has happened only you all will be able to tell me, but what I can say is that some schemes have emerged out of this which are addressing these issues.

When this report came in 1995, my personal assessment is that the press has not taken as much note of it as it should have. It has valuable information. On the basis of the statistics in the report we could have exposed a lot of things in the state as well as in the country. Not only is the administration, the press is also responsible for it. The report was made available to all in MP and also in Delhi. It might have secondary data but it is still important.

3
Crisis to Chaos

Sudeep Banerjee
Principal, Secretary, Madhya Pradesh

I would like to begin my presentation at the workshop with some basic demographic data of the Hindi speaking areas, that is, the four main states of Madhya Pradesh, Bihar, Uttar Pradesh and Rajasthan. If we see the statistics in their totality on birth rate, infant mortality rate, death rate and literacy not only are they different from the rest of the country, but they are even worse than the world's most difficult areas, the sub-Saharan Africa.

It is our great fortune that in these Hindi speaking areas a state of civil war does not exist as it does in the sub-Saharan states. As you can see, we are able to get together here and discuss the situation as it pertains to the administration, the press and the public. But all the preconditions exist here which may yet lead to a civil war situation. In fact, let me point out that we are passing through a phase of low intensity civil conflict and the atmosphere is so vitiated and fluid that anything may happen at any time. Mention has been made of tension between the press and the administration.

This is not wholly correct as there are points of collaboration between the two which express themselves in certain situations and in their respective assessment of specific situations. The press does not always look at conflict situations from the point of view of the adivasis. Nor does the administration. The attitude of the press and the administration seems to be one mutually reinforcing each other's approach.

For instance, a great deal has appeared in the press about armed conflicts in Khargaon among adivasis and their organisations like the *Adivasi Mukti Sanghatana* and the *Adivasi Samaj Sudhar Shanti Sena.* I have nothing to say about the rights and wrongs of these and the other groups involved in the conflict but what seems pertinent to me is that the press is more interested in projecting these conflicts as widely as possible rather than in writing about conditions in the area of which these conflicts are but a symptom.

Thus, I have not come across an investigative report on how much land has been lost by the adivasis and to whom in the last fifty years of independence. It is not as if it requires much in-depth research on the part of journalists to ascertain data on this issue all of which is readily available with the administration's research units. Yet there is no analysis to find out whether this refusal to come face to face with grim reality may well get completely out of hand. This may well be because both the media and the administration is manned by people from a strata of society which cannot see the issues from the perspective of the adivasis.

If we are not alert in the next few years, our social and political conditions would deteriorate to the pattern of the situation in sub-Saharan Africa though for the time being there seems to be scope enough for improvements which can lead to the reconciliation of conflicts and contradictions gripping the region. It is necessary for media persons to anticipate a possible catastrophe as much as the possibility of heading it off which presents itself and respond appropriately.

It is not as though there is much effort that has to be put in to marshal evidence to bring about an awareness of the implications of the two options opening out to the public and the urgency to deal decisively with the situation. The first step which both the press and the administration need to take is to evolve a consensus on what should be done to arrest the deterioration of the situation further. It so happens that neither the media nor the administration differ on the grim situation. Neither have they so far seem to have evolved an approach to find a solution to it.

Thus what Sainath has written in the last one year there is not much difference between the press and the administration about poverty and hunger in these areas. Social scientists and economists have been bringing out for some time now that during five years of economic success, per capita availability of food grains has gone down. But what are the behavioral implications of this? These are not being looked at either by the press or the administration. A lot of economists and a lot of issues of the Economic and Political Review are full of these statistics and nobody is challenging these statistics. There is not even a protest from the administration about such statistics where one is saying that 10 died and another is saying five had died.

In this country if the availability of food becomes less for the poor its behavioural implications are dramatic but the press hardly takes any notice of it. The claim by Amartya Sen about famine studies in India in the last 10 to 15 years is that India has no famines similar to those in China. He has attributed this to the fact that there is an independent press in India. The second thing he said, however, was that we have ignored chronic hunger in India. In China there have been a lot of big famines during this time but the country does not have a situation of chronic hunger. Both the countries started with the same life expectancy of 50 years. It is 70 in China and 60 in India. There is general agreement about them. There is no conflict about the statistics and about these realities. The economists are all right. Yet everybody is quiet and unmoved by the human suffering the situation entails. In between some people like Sainath and other small newspapers talk about these things. They are carrying on some kind of a crusade. For everyone, his role is governed by a struggle.

The basis for what I have said is not only what I have seen personally, it is secondary evidence which I have read in newspapers and from academic readings. We have people in large numbers who are making efforts at all levels so that these things come into notice. In such difficult situations there are people in the press who have been doing good work and even better and more valiant work is being done in the academic circle. I have one request that though we may not be able to see everything at the grassroots why can't we see the voluminous work being brought out by people in academics? Why are we ignoring this? If you see issues like tribal situation or more recently in Khargaon and Khanwar or about Bastar or the Narmada Bachao Andolan you will feel that though the work is not very much but those in academics have collected a lot of material. There is a lot of analysis.

There is a tension between academics and the press. Academics want to take time in saying something and those in the press want the information by tomorrow and whatever journalists can get by then is the truth. But if we do not go so much into the principles but discuss it as an informed alternative then this is a practical suggestion that if academicians, sociologists, economists and political scientists are brought together in forums to discuss these things then both they and the press can benefit from it. This is ten times more true for the administration as well. We people do not benefit at all from academics. We do not read books because we feel that we have passed the exams so we need not read more. Our knowledge has stopped there.

All that I am saying about the press, please assume that it is much more true of the administration. We have access to libraries and books but we still do not read them. Everybody has opinions, people want to establish a lot of things but they do not want to read what other people have done. A hatred for books and academics also is responsible for this gap. If we can improve this then we can have a practical solution to the problem but how do we get newspapers and journalists to focus on this? It is not as if they will have to work extra hard to look for these things. All that they have to do is to pay more attention to what is already visible.

Coming to the administration and its relationship with the press, the first point to note is that the administration is a monolith only for the sake of argument. If I am asked my opinion about the press and journalists then I cannot say anything in the abstract. I remember some faces and I want to say some things about some and other things about others. The same is true of the administration. Because of backwardness, because of the non development of institutions, the administration has been given rigid roles. It is not like this. Our administration or even our South Block is not like Pentagon. It is porous. There are 50 kinds of stratifications. Because of a lack of development our system is already transparent. There is so much of transparency everywhere which we can use but the people are trying to make it opaque as well. More than half the government officials are fighting against the administration as well. They are a part of the government but they are also waging a war against it. The higher you go, for instance if you go to Vallabh Bhavan you will see that the people are in a tussle. The situation is not so monolithic that it is daunting to the press.

In Delhi you write in your paper that 'this is Shastri Bhavan's point of view' so you feel that a building like Shastri Bhavan has only one opinion. But if you go inside there will be so many differences of opinion even within one department and people will be ready to talk to you in a frank manner. There is no Shastri Bhavan view. This myth has been created by the press — Shastri Bhavan has a view about the Prasar Bharati Bill, etc. These short cut methods of reporting are right in their own place but when we start believing in them ourselves and start operating as if these categories exist in reality then it becomes problematic. Otherwise our system is sufficiently vulnerable today for any average journalist to dig out as much information as he wants to. It has not become so opaque that it is difficult to operate it. You will find that the people because of a variety of reasons, or just to be nice, want to tell you the truth if you go out to the field.

I don't know if Sainath has mentioned it but I believe that quite a bit of information must have come from officials. Whenever you approach an official he does not believe that the entire government machinery rests on his shoulders. He meets you in an individual capacity. This is possible in a less developed society. In western countries (I have dealt with the more advanced bureaucracies) it is impossible to make people talk off the record. It is impossible to make them talk about anything other than the view of the organisation they are representing.

S.C. Behar
Former Chief Secretary, Government of Madhya Pradesh.
Presently adviser to the Chief Minister.

Responding to a series of comments on the functioning of the administration and answering queries was the presentation for Behar. "I agree that there is a lot of distance between the press and the administration. I also agree that the press cannot believe most of the things that the administration says. I also believe that the press is justified in having such an attitude. However, the administration has a lot of problems which I would like to share with you. I have a number of premises, first about the administration.

The first premise is that there is a misconception about the administration: that it is responsible for the world and the nation. That it is omnipotent and omniscient. Sadly this misconception is perpetuated by everybody, including the press. When there is a boat tragedy in Hoshangabad, the administration is attacked immediately. The administration starts feeling that it is responsible for the tragedy. I feel this is very significant. Ever since I have been in the administration (now I am marginalised) I have believed that you have to understand your limitations. The problem is that nobody accepts their limitations - neither us or them. You feel that I am responsible for everything and am answerable to you, so you attack me. Instead of saying that it was the fault of the infrastructure and this has been continuing for a while there is a personalised attack. So I also go on the defensive instead of presenting you with the truth.

What I feel is a big problem is that the people in the administration have a huge ego. It is very difficult to curb this ego. I have tried for so many years to reduce it. There is no doubt about this. But if you will excuse me I would like to say that the press too played a role here. If it had been slightly less the problem would not have arisen.

Let me put it another way, I'll place the IAS in front it will become easier. When a journalist writes he thinks he knows everything. Likewise, an IAS official or a person from the administration too thinks the same. This is the ego and this is the problem.

An open mind does not exist either amongst colleagues or in the administration or in most of the journalists. The administration is a closed system and that is a problem. You are concerned about transparency in this system but there is another problem. The closed system is such that the person who makes a mistake can never be punished. When there is a complaint against a *thanedar* invariably instead of a proper inquiry, the inquiry either reaches the *thanedar* himself or the circle officer above him whom he knows and the two share a personal relationship so we never get to know the truth. It is a closed system.

When the administration gives some statistics, you want the right figures and if there is a mistake you criticize it. But when a journalist writes, he can give any figure. It is not understood that when an accident happens it takes time for the figures to be ascertained. We are not omniscient, we are not omnipotent. We are trying to look at the situation in the best possible way in that small timeframe.

The respect that is given to instant news rather than the truth is a big problem according to me. Giving news immediately is important because there is competition. It is assumed that giving the right news three days later is wrong but I should give whatever news I have tomorrow is right. The problem here is that when it is a big tragedy not everything is known-neither I know it and nor do you. If you accept that I am telling you whatever I have in the given circumstances then the problems can be solved.

As Sainath said yesterday it is good that there should be tension between the press and the administration, it is a good statement. The tension must remain. But what kind of tension? Is it a tension of competitors or is it a tension of adversaries? I think it is of competitors, not of adversaries. Who runs the government and who runs the press? Who decides the policies of the government and who decides those of the press? When we talk of the common man, to what extent are competition factors operating and to what extent are our real objectives operating?

Both of them have the same objective improving the lot of the people. But I had learnt early on in life that objectives are of two types: professed and real. Isn't it true that whether the press or the government talk about the benefit of the people both are primarily competing for standing in society. What are the reasons for the press becoming anti-establishment?

This is its way of getting its rights. If the BJP is in power we should be anti-establishment, if the Congress is in power then also we should be anti-establishment. The day I become pro establishment I will lose the game.

The society is heterogeneous and the people who matter in it are the influential ones, it is the elite group, the *avjatya* group which is fighting for power. The real thing is that nobody is bothered about the happiness and sorrow of the common man, but only to an extent that it serves your purpose can make this. Thus it is essentially a tool, a pawn in your power game. That is why the neglected sectors are not just neglected by the press. They are also neglected by the government.

Those who are not from MP will probably not know this but I had really pleaded that the government officials should go and spend three days in a village and in those villages which do not have guest houses. And secondly, they would have to go alone and not without their junior officers. Thirdly, you will not go there with the help of the *patel, patwari*. You will go on your own so that you can have direct contact with the poor people. We are talking about a heterogeneous society and if you will go with the help of those who are oppressing others, how will you get to know the truth?

I was talking about power games in the neglected sector with a specific purpose. If it is a rural area it is neglected, if it is a marginalised group it is neglected. They are neglected both by the government as well as the press. For the welfare of the scheduled castes, scheduled tribes, there are separate committees at the state level. I have attended countless meetings of these. Eighty per cent of the time in these meetings is devoted finding out to whether scheduled caste and scheduled tribe officials are getting due promotions, whether recruitments are going on or not. They only want to know about promotion and recruitment. Basically it is a fight between the elite classes and the other, and not between the press and the administration. Even the SC and ST people who are coming forward want to see what all the elite classes can get.

Can it be a constructive relationship between the press and the administration? I agree that there has to be tension, but shouldn't it also be constructive? Why aren't we able to do something. May be my policymakers are such that they do not allow me. But there are decision makers in the press as well. I'll give you a small example. When I became the chief secretary I was praised a lot. Later on I was criticised also. The press has the right to falsely praise me and also falsely criticise me. But there is a newspaper group (I will not name it) which was very appreciative but in a particular month, it started writing against me. I know when I am in public life, I will be criticised because everybody will not like what I say, there will be differences. This paper used to write with so much of wit and satire that you could say nothing, but you could make out that it is negative. I had paid no attention to it at first, but later I figured out that the owner of the paper wanted to get something done from me through the chief minister and I had pointblank refused to do it. Since then the attitude of the paper changed.

The interesting thing is that the editors of the paper are still my friends. But it was the policy of the house that the chief secretary should be painted slightly black. They could not do very much because I have negative as well as positive qualities.

We have had in-house discussions on the relationship between the press and the administration. I have formed a group to devise ways and means of improving this relationship and the government. The first is transparency. I agree with this totally. I had formed a law for transparency. I went to the Press Council first and then the Chief Minister went to the Press Council and said that the law that they had made for transparency was incomplete and that there should be more transparency.

But when I made the law, you can't imagine how difficult it was to convince my principal secretaries and ultimately when that went to the cabinet even a diluted draft was not passed, and was submitted to a cabinet sub-committee. Twentyfour departments in Madhya Pradesh have given orders for transparency. But I am not satisfied with this and you should not praise it because there are two views about transparency.

The first one is that everything should come under transparency except in certain areas and areas in which transparency is permitted have been listed. But I have been agitating for total transparency and in this I have been having a clash with the members of my own academy. My faculty members are extremely reluctant.

I would like to say two more things on transparency which I have been fighting about for long. It is inappropriate to look at transparency only in the context of the administration. It is needed equally in the press and in the banks. Why does a bank insist on maintaining the confidence of the customer? What is there in my money that it needs to be hidden? Why shouldn't the bank be transparent? Why shouldn't the press be transparent. You may not give the source as it may dry up but there is a basis for your writing and if somebody asks for that basis, why shouldn't you give it?

In private companies there should be transparency in everything except trade secrets which lead to competition. My problem is that when we start fighting against only the government about transparency it takes an ostrich-like approach. It tries to hide things. This argument has been given to me by my faculty that you are transparent, but what about the others? If you decide to implement transparency in the entire society then we will let you implement it here as well. When others hide things why do you want to show everything?

Why is there a desire to hide? I think there are two reasons for this: there are no value based decisions. If there is favouritism involved like say I am giving money for irrigation, where the percentage of irrigation facilities is high and not in that district where it is low, and as it is a non-value based decision so you try to hide it. This is the fault of our system. There is a lot of favouritism in our system. That is the reason why there should be transparency forcibly imposed so that there are no non value-based decisions.

Shukla who was the minister told me repeatedly, "What do you mean only we favour people. Don't you people from the administration also indulge in favouritism." He was right. Even we indulge in favouritism whenever we get a chance. This is one big reason and this is because of our system.

In the relationship between the press and the administration I want to see in the press a reward and punishment system. In the government this system does not work well. It does not operate properly. But will you be able to encourage good people and discourage the bad ones? We cannot come in directly but we would like to help you so that the truth comes out. But if we start feeling that the press respects the right people and does not respect the wrong ones, it does not appreciate those who give gifts but those who do not give gifts then I think it will be a big help.

Sainath: I found myself slightly out of tune with one part of the discussion. I agree that there should be tension between the press and the administration. But much of the time I worry about the press getting too close to the administration. The problem is that the press is in bed with the administration in many parts of the country and I think this is also a problem that we need to discuss.

I think there is too much dependence on official sources and also within official sources there seems to be dependence on individual official sources rather than the establishment flow of information. I think there has to be a multiplicity of sources, whether in history or archaeology. You need to look for corroborative sources so that you don't have to take only one person's version. The people themselves, in the context of rural reporting, is an ocean of sources for journalists.

The most underutilised sources in this country is the use of already published information. I think we need to engineer a marriage between reporting and social sciences. There is a lot of available information and I think with one little thing we can change the perspective apart from right to information and legislation which has its limits. If we realise that the kind of sources and information we seek is related to the kind of stories. If we realise that the press is there to signal the weaknesses in society, that it is there to ring the bell and in rural reporting to give a voice to the marginalised then I think our perspective about what sources we need and use would undergo radical changes.

Behar: I agree with what Sainath has said. It was beyond my purview to discuss what other means of information are available to us, other than the government. He has spoken about marginalised groups in society. I agree with him that this is a major source which we do not tap.

The second thing which I want to discuss further is the availability of documents with the government. If we start reading them and drawing conclusions from them we will have a lot of information. The problem is that we do not see these documents, we only listen to what is told to us. If you start reading a document, you will get a lot of information.

Thirdly, he is right when he says that there is too much dependence on the government. I feel there should be more dependence and in this context I had started something which I consider another aspect of tranparency. By asking any question in the Vidhan Sabha you can get information. A resourceful person gets a question asked in the Vidhan Sabha, he gets the information and this is printed in the papers. So what confidentiality are we talking about when the information is available so easily? But when you ask for information directly you do not get it. I have tried to give directions to officials at district and divisional levels that any information which has to be given via an MLA or MP should be given directly. The only problem is that this is not complied information so I have asked these officials to give whatever they have by way of copies otherwise they will have to give it via the Vidhan Sabha.

For the time being, the information with the Vidhan Sabha is also a big source. We do not need to go anywhere else.

Another thing which has not been discussed today is corruption. I feel very strongly about this as well and for me giving one person an out of turn job as a favour is as big a corrupt act as taking money. But we do not look at this because the definition of corruption has been restricted to money. I feel that the relationship between the press and the administration should not be one of cooption. You have seen how successfully the press has been coopted in Madhya Pradesh, what kind of favours have been given to members of the press because of which many of them are not being truthful in their reporting.

Q: You have just said that by asking a question in the Vidhan Sabha you can get any information you want. My experience is different. The bureaucracy has taught the ministers how not to give information. For three sessions, we were told that information was being collected.

Behar: You are right when you say that they delay the matter by saying that the information is being collected. But once it is collected, the information has to be given. I would like to remind you that it is only a question of patience.

In oral questions also there is a lot of scope of hiding information. But let me give you an example. If you ask did such a thing happen on 28.9.97? I say no, because the event took place either a day earlier or a day later. It is a different matter that some like me say that it did not happen on the 28th but on the 27th. While a lot is hidden during the oral discussions, there is a lot of information in the printed matter. As Sainath has said can you take a cue and investigate further? If you do that, then you will find a lot of interesting details.

4

A Challenge Met

S R Hiremath

An environmental activist based in Harihar, northern Karnataka.

I am working with an environmental group called the Samaj Parivartan Samudaya in North Karnataka. I was involved in an integrated rural development work in some of the villages of Karnataka and we had to tackle the problem of pollution of Tungbhandra river caused by two Birla industries, Harihar Polyfibres and Grasim industries. A widespread notion prevalent among villagers with whom I had worked for five years was that Birlas were too powerful in the country with ministers, officials and even members of Parliament in their pockets and so there was very little that we could do. This was the kind of despondency and despair among the people.

Moreover, at that time we were having a very bad experience with the Ministry of Environment and Forests because we were asking them for land costing about Rs 50,000 to conduct a scientific study on the pollution of the Tungbhadra river. The first question a scientific officer of the ministry asked us was, "Who owns that industry?" Our reply was that it was a Birla group industry. Promptly he told us: "Forget it. There is very little chance that you will get any money from the ministry." He also warned us that the Birlas were too powerful and even if he put up a proposal for giving us the land, it would take so long that we would only be disappointed and nothing would come out of it.

I asked him for his suggestions and he said that we should go to the state government. He also told us that we had a chance if we spoke to V Balasubramaniam, then secretary to the Chief Minister, who was known to be an upright officer and sympathetic to grassroots organisations.

When I spoke to him, his first question was, "Do you mind getting money from the pollution control board itself?" That was a strange question because as far as I knew the money came from the budget allocation of the state government. When I told him I did not mind, he said that he would send the proposal. He asked me how we were planning to attack the problem. According to him, in this kind of struggle we needed to link up with good people in various sectors particularly in the media because when crucial, large scale fish-kill takes place letting off pollutants into the river it causes havoc with the fish and also the fields. We needed to get to know people in the media who could expose this.

I thought this was a very perceptive statement on his part. I asked him for names of some mediapersons and he named Mr. Madan Mohan of the *Hindu* in Hubli. And since then this has served us as a very important advice. Since then we have gained a lot of credibility and trust among the media group in Hubli which has stood us in good stead as this struggle advanced. Within three to four years we had a great deal of impact on the pollution control board, the government of Karnataka, on the officials because of the positive role of media. Having said that, I would like to also say that unless you have comprehensive coverage, the issues do not go very far.

For example, in summer months when the flow of the river is lean and the intensity of the pollution is very high, considerable fish-kill takes place. One of the suggestions repeatedly made by villagers was that why this industry was allowed to take water from upstream and not downstream. They pointed out that if this was done then they would have to treat the affluents for meeting requirements of law if not in deference to the needs of the villagers. Another suggestion of the villagers was that the pollution control board regional officers were far away from where the pollution is intense and that they should be downstream. Though these were useful suggestions, and there had even been struggles of people over these ideas, they did not attract adequate media projection although havoc which pollution, a by-product of so called industrial development played with the livelihood of vast sections of the people on both sides of the river as well as in the interior because of air pollution caused by the plants was great.

Among the journalists we first met was Ajit Bhattacharjea who first of all wanted to visit the fields. One of our consistent requests to the press had been that only when journalists visited the area and met people living there, they would be in a position to understand the full impact of the pollution. The field visit becomes an inexhaustible source of information and learning to journalists, a few of whom did so, to us it contributes immensely to out struggle. After visiting the areas and after detailed discussions Bhattacharjea wrote a series of articles in *The Deccan Herald* opening the eyes of legislators and also of the media and a number of papers began to take notice. All this acted as a catalyst in crystallising public opinion which eventually forced the state government to come out decisively in our favour.

Coming to our more recent experience in Bastar district. This has to do with what the previous collector of Bastar called the timber mafia. This mafia consists of selected members from the bureaucracy, from the political sphere and the timber merchants themselves. From the political sphere it is a who's who of influential people from Bastar.

The modus operandi of the timber mafia is that a timber merchant concludes a *benami* deal with a tribal. Another tribal buys land and the trees on it from this tribal and it is the trees which are important. In the 50s, when the government of MP gave land to tribals for their ownership, it also gave the ownership of the valuable trees to these tribals. These trees vary from fruit trees to sagwani to sesham. For example a sagwani tree costs between Rs. 40,000 to Rs. 90,000, depending on the maturity and the size of the girth.

The mafia buys the land with the trees at throwaway prices and then obtains permission from the district administration to fell the trees. There is a lot of corruption involved here. Then they go and fell the trees with the help of the forest department. And since these are nationalised trees the forest department literally hands over the cheques. These cheques were handed for Rs. 48 lakh and Rs. 17 lakh to Mahendra Karma, former MP. This is how they make money.

We filed a public interest litigation and the Supreme Court ordered an inquiry into this scandal by the Lokayukta of Uttar Pradesh. The interim report on five specific villages and the cases involved therein was submitted on July 5, 1997. Last December the sealed covers were opened.

One of the things which the judges took very serious note of was of a transaction in village Badeguda. There 29 tribals got Rs. 1,20,000 and 849 trees worth Rs. 3 crore was bought by six persons led by Virendra Netam, brother of Arvind and Shiv Netam. The Additional Collector gave permission for only 130 trees and on that they appealed to the Commissioner, Narayan Singh, the kingpin of the officialdom and a very significant actor of this timber mafia and he gave permission for 849 trees.

What was unusual about this situation was that the Collector of Bastar district, P Rajgopalan Naidu wrote three well documented letters to the government of MP saying this is how the timber mafia operates and these are the powerful forces involved.

He wrote these three letters and the government did not heed much of his advise about how to deal with the situation. It was at this time that the intervention from the Samaj Parivartan Samudaya came in the form of an interlocutory application in a major forest matter which is before the Supreme Court in writ petition number 202 of 1995.

One of the reasons we chose this option was because of Prashant Bhushan's advice to us that this was simpler and cost much less. Supreme Court, division bench headed by Justice J S Verma who comes from MP took serious note of it and immediately issued an order banning felling of trees in Bastar and asking the government to file a report within two weeks of actions taken. Needless to say he was disappointed by the action taken and the report given by the government.

Then he ordered the Lokayukta inquiry on 5th March and both of these decisions were important decisions in making a beginning in terms of unearthing the scandal and laying before the nation how a timber mafia operates which is the same in Bastar and in Kalahandi in Orissa or Andhra Pradesh or anywhere else. So this has very serious national implications.

The media has taken an interest in this off and on. For example, the local paper, *Deshbandhu* which has correspondents in Bastar was the first one to take serious note of this scandal and to give good publicity. The third letter of Rajgopal Naidu showed that Narayan Singh, his boss and commissioner of Bastar really gave a corrupt orientation to his department, which he had documented in his letter alongwith enclosures which laid bare how he was involved in this scandal.

This was a front page story in *Deshbandhu* but very few national papers took note of this. But when we got into the picture, the first and the second order in our favour also did not get much immediate coverage but many journalists to whom we sent the material made this into a news report. We have been requesting journalist to visit the place but few have done so.

The Lokayukta reports have a tremendous volume of information: how the timber mafia operates, how the officers fell in line and did not visit the field. Another important aspect of the modus operandi is taking advantage of old records. When land was given to the *bhumiswamis*, they were adjacent to the state owned forest lands so what the patwari does is that when one tribal buys land from another tribal it is shown by the revenue inspector as state-owned land on paper. For example, in the Netam family case only 130 trees are on the land of the tribals. The rest of the 849 are on state owned forest land. And this was true even of all other transactions. This means that they are systematically looting not only the tribals but also the state owned forests. Many of you know that the recent forest survey of India report says that 4,995 square kilometers of forests have disappeared in MP alone.

What we are talking about are sizeable operations. The second modus operandi, which we have linked up with this has to do with the so-called allotment of government land to non-tribal landless people. These lands also have trees worth crores of rupees growing on them.

For example in 1991 when Sudeep Banerjee was Commissioner of Bastar he filed criminal cases against non-tribals and also his own officials like tehsildars who allotted government land with trees worth millions of rupees in violation of laws. A sarpanch in Dandewada area of Bastar district got land allotted to his four children. His unmarried daughter who was allotted five acres of land, had trees worth Rs. 15 lakh. And these are rich people and by no stretch of imagination eligible for allotment of land under landless category. More than 3,000 criminal cases filed against non tribals are languishing in cold storage there.

The Digvijay Singh government is yet to revive these cases. Also because of the pressure due to the work we are doing and a number of honest IAS officers the cases have been revived. 1,300 cases have been identified and the land has been reverted to the government but what we told the collector was that it is not the land, it is the trees.

This is the magnitude of the scandal which they are trying to do "legally" which are blatantly illegal. The third modus operandi is illegal felling and this is where Shiv Netam is playing a central role in the northern part of Bastar. We conducted a lot of studies here and thanks to good forest officers who showed a lot of interest we went for spot inspection and we have produced a 93-page report. Ashok Desai, Attorney General of India, who had known the earlier case suggested we file this with the Supreme Court of India which we have done.

We made three prayers to the Supreme Court on 5th January. The first prayer concerned what Rajgopal identified involving the three year period of Narayan Singh, which has more than 2,000 cases and the time of Sudip Banerji where too 3,000 cases are involved. The land should be restored to the tribals, the true value of the trees established and criminal charges initiated against those who got these by violating the laws, and also punitive damages to the people should be given. All this should be done under the overall supervision of the Lokayukta because you don't trust the government which has failed to do its duties earlier.

The third prayer was to order a CBI inquiry and use all the links to find out the role of the politicians and also timber merchants who operate in the background, providing finance, etc. but are not involved in the transactions. Fortunately, the Supreme Court heard these and the CBI inquiry has begun.

This we felt was a significant order but media coverage was very partial. Some journalists covered it very well but most did not. The harassment of the tribals and activists in the area, which took place in front of the Lokayukta committee. This involves distribution of money to tribals and threatening them with dire consequences, abusing Rajgopal Naidu and Ratnashekar Nath.

Recently the harassment and the arrest of one of our activists in custody has not been taken note of by the local media. But we informed some national journalists about it, who wrote about it.

Finally, before concluding I would like to say there has been a positive response of the media in these matters. Though the media coverage has been fair, I think some communication gap exists. I think in our over-enthusiasm we did not pay heed to feed the kind of information and the angle from which journalists could see it in a systematic way. I hope this workshop will throw light as to how we can provide this information and how journalists can use it. But I would like to emphasise again on the need for journalists for spot visits and meeting the people.

Bharat Dogra

An activist and a freelance journalist

I have been working on these issues for the last two decades and I started writing in English to begin with and have started writing in Hindi more recently. My experience has not been a very happy one. When I compare the conditions today to what they were when I started writing I feel that there were more opportunities then of getting these stories published in the national papers.

But in the last four-five years I do not have the confidence that if I put in a lot of work, which I have to do as a freelance journalist, the stories will be published properly in the national papers. On the other hand, I find Hindi newspapers more receptive, that there is more space particularly on edit pages for these kind of stories. But on the whole, however, the space for this kind of writing has been diminishing. There was a time when newspapers had separate pages for development and environment.

While we can plan in various ways how more of such writing has to be done, and in a better way we also need to think about convincing editors that they should devote more space to such stories.

I have also been teaching some journalism students development and environment journalism and I find that they are very idealistic and want to do this kind of work. I have had a good response from them but when I meet them after three or four years they have lost much of their idealism. They tell me that they tried writing about themes related to development but when they did not get much encouragement they had to change. This is very sad that within four-five years, students lose their idealism.

Hiremath has given us various examples but I think at times we tend to forget the other side: that of the role of the media. Several grassroots organisations which have done a lot of good work and have not hesitated to challenge the administration have also complained that the press operated against them. This phenomenon has been ignored by us for a very long time.

I would like to give one example which is from the Raipur press in the Chattisgarh area. One movement which I have tried to cover from the very beginning is the Chattisgarh Mine Shramik Sangathan led by the late Shiv Shankar Guha Niyogi. I have been covering this for 15 years and during this period whenever I visited the Chattisgarh area the movement was facing some crisis. One of the main problems which they were faced with was the unsympathetic role of the press. And they would show me mounds of clippings on how the press published what the industrialists gave them and never their point of view. Even if there was a small disagreement amongst the activists it would become front page news. If there was some small retaliatory violence by the activists the press would say that they had been trained in China, that they are Naxalites. These clippings were then used to release repression against the organisation.

The irony of the situation was that the journalists who were doing these stories at the behest of the vested interests were being given awards for development journalism. I was also recipient of the same award with another journalist and I knew how he had been selected. Later I saw him spend the money he had got on liquor and that sort of things. This is another face of the press.

Later I was covering the struggles of industrial workers in Faridabad, Ghaziabad and other places. Again I noticed that problems related to health, the very serious health problems they faced were never highlighted. On the other hand, what industrialists had to say was highlighted. I think newspapers have this tendency that if a reporter is covering some wrong doing in a remote region of Bastar district, that would be highlighted as a big example of development journalism but in neighbouring Faridabad if some industrialists are killing workers that will not be reported because these industrialists were also giving advertisements to the papers.

I fully endorse the view that development journalism should be supported but at the same time we should not forget that so many trade unions and genuine grassroots organisations have complaints against the press. Sometimes, they are operating in such difficult conditions and they do not have educated people and their genuine problems need to be highlighted.

The other aspect is development news yes, but what sort of development news? On the one hand there is that development news which questions existing establishment myths and actually gives support to the grassroots struggles and on the other hand there is another kind of development news which actually strengthens the big contractors and industrialists against whom the struggles are being conducted. There can be for example a lot of articles that have been written justifying the construction of large dam projects and also justifying a lot of other mega projects which are known to be very harmful. These journalists are very highly respected and they have been continuously writing against the struggles and in favour of the mega projects and it needs to be discussed whether this sort of developmental journalism is what we want more newspapers space for.

In fact this is one aspect which, I think has been most neglected in the entire debate on questioning the existing paradigm of development and raising questions on what exactly development is. And also raising inconvenient questions where exactly the existing development path has taken you including the richest nations and those countries which are dictating the development path presently to us and what does it have in store for us.

Actually the biggest pillars of the development establishments themselves admit now that the environmental crisis has become so acute that this itself can be used as a very powerful argument against the development pattern that has been followed so far. But this is not reflected adequately in the newspapers and actually in a way I think the newspapers actually promote consumerism. In fact I think the entire media promotes consumerism, whereas I think the basic crisis of existing development is consumerism, that the more you promote consumerism you cannot even talk about environmental protection.

So our newspapers on the one hand promote consumerism fully and on the other hand they say two or three nice things about environment protection. I think there is a lot of hypocrisy in this. And those who are not interested in getting just a few articles published but are genuinely interested in the media playing a relevant role in telling people really what environment protection means and development ought to be , I think have really a lot of hard thinking to do and as Hiremathji was saying in a particular struggle we can get the newspapers to write a few articles and features I have also been involved with several movements and in my own way have tried that when these movements were on to get a few stories published and that has happened.

But on the bigger question of what development is, where we are headed for or what is really environment protection, I find, it difficult to persuade newspapers to support us.

5

Trends in the Hindi Press

Ajit Bhattacharjea
Director, Press Institute of India

One of the deplorable lapses in the English press, particularly those in newspapers brought out in the metropolitan centres, is the absence of reportage of rural life. One hardly comes across any worthwhile descriptive or analytical story on how people in the rural areas live and what their problems are unless there is a calamity, man made or otherwise. Yet 75 per cent of our people live in rural areas which provide livelihood for the bulk of our population. This is a slur on the English press.

This should not, and need not, be so. The fact remains, however, that most Hindi papers, with few exceptions, have modelled themselves on the metro-oriented elitist English press. The front pages of these papers have more or less the same items and, by and large, they have not evolved their own identity. This is the subject which Prabash Joshi has been striving after and has done his own bit in changing this trend.

This calls for an orientation for the Hindi press which has to be uniquely its own and its quest has to be a continuous process. Hopefully this workshop will be the beginning of this process. Before we take on this challenging task, it would be useful for us to take a look at the present state of the Hindi press so that we can identify the direction in which we should move.

Ravindra Shukla
Nai Duniya, Indore

I think it is inappropriate to compare the coverage given to what is happening in villages in Hindi and English newspapers. Most Hindi newspapers cover what is of importance in the villages. Be it *Nai Duniya* or any other paper, three or four pages are devoted to this coverage. But the question is not one of quantity but of quality. The quality should be so good that the administration's focus is shifted to the conditions and something is done about them.

Nai Duniya has given importance to collecting information about the villages ever since it was set up. The paper had organised two workshops in 1970 on this subject. A need was felt for this because the reporters covering villages do not have news sense.

We have guidelines for rural coverage in *Nai Duniya*. The focus for these has been on both the reporters and the stringers. The stringers also do not have any news sense. We have attempted to send them proformas from time to time asking them what they can do to cover a particular event, who all they can interview, where they can go for additional information. We are doing this on a regular basis.

In 1983 when I returned from a workshop in Manila, we decided to publish a four page supplement called *Anchalik Vishesh*. In this we covered events which touch our everyday lives in villages. In *Nai Duniya*, we have always focussed on agriculture and we gave this subject even more importance in *Anchalik Vishesh*.

We simplified what the experts had to say so that even the common farmer could understand it. We also came up with a vocabulary and emphasised on the fact that whatever was being written should be understood by the farmers. The experts had problems finding appropriate words in Hindi for terms like insecticides and pesticides, or for names of diseases, etc.

The experts also had a problem with translations because they felt we would change the meaning of what they were saying when we translated it. But we managed to get their confidence and they allowed us to translate their works.

On the other hand we also inspired farmers to let us know about their problems. We asked them to write their problems to the correspondents so that we could direct the correspondents to take appropriate action. We got a very good response for this from lots of farmers — some were class 7 pass, some were matric pass but they all were inspired to write about their villages.

However the problem we faced was that most of them concentrated on the same things — no roads, no water, etc. But at times we got a lot of insight into the culture and society of the villages. We managed to generate a lot of rural writers and we benefited a lot from them.

What I also did was to go and speak to a farmer in a village and then published what he had to say in an interview format with his photograph. This generated a lot of interest in what he was saying and also gave his problem credibility. These techniques were picked up by others and hence it also managed to inspire others to take the initiative. The question that arises now is: how can we make such schemes more widespread. If these small attempts are made by more newspapers we will be able to understand the villages much better.

The first step in any such work is taken by the editors. They should take more initiatives to start such things in their papers. If the problem is one of the right techniques to be adopted, we can organise more workshops.

Another question which arises is: should we have some guidelines for this? Let me admit that it would be very tough to come up with the guidelines but we can try. But what I would like to say is that the trend in newspapers is focussing less on professionalism and more on its being a profession. In such a scenario, any guidelines that we come up with are not going to be very effective.

Vijay Sahgal
Editor, Dainik Tribune

I am glad the Press Institute has taken this first step in focussing attention to such an important subject. It is a pity that only politics makes news. But I would like to tell you that we have started focussing on villages in *Dainik Tribune.* Two of our attempts have been quite successful.

The first of this was the Postcard Correspondent. We carried a notice in our paper that if you know how to read or write and if you have any problem, you can write to us about it in 50 words. We started this as news from villages. This was followed by other papers as well. The second attempt was *Gaon ki Kahani.* We publish about 700 words with pictures on what the village is now and how does it compares with the past.

What I would focus on is that newspapers should devote some pages to news from villages. Even in papers coming from Delhi there should be some space, even if it is only one column. If it is done, it would be a big help. Some universities have courses on rural reporting by the UGC. Some of these have not been accepted but they are operational in others. There should be jobs in our newspapers for trained people coming out of these universities. For all other streams there are openings but there are none for journalists trained in rural reporting.

Moreover, we should try and speak the language of the villagers. In Haryana, two years ago I found out about an insect which destroys *kapas*. It is called *American sundi.* We published a lot of reports on this — and its harmful effects, where it came from and what could be done to prevent it.

Ramakant Goswami
Chief Reporter, Dainik Hindustan, Delhi

I feel that very few of us sitting here — I am referring to those of us from metropolitan centres — have done rural reporting and for that matter would like to. Most of the reporters would in fact consider a posting to rural areas to be a punishment posting. Now, however, the situation is changing. Today there is competition amongst newspapers. *Punjab Kesri* is selling more than mine is. The Delhi culture is a very Punjabi culture so they want to read what *Punjab Kesri* writes. People from MP want to read a paper from there. All people from UP want to read *Dainik Jagran*. So when *Dainik Hindustan* is surrounded from all the sides we have to look for newer options. Now even we have started focussing on the rural areas but our concentration is on urban villages because all the new colonies in Delhi are coming up on villages. So their problems are those of the villages. There is a lot of similarity between the problems in the villages and cities.

All Hindi papers in Delhi have started a dharma page. We have started giving columns to this and we have reporters specialising in this religious reporting. I feel that if you have to survive you have to have this kind of marketing approach.

It is definite that Hindi newspapers are increasing but journalists working for these papers need to get rid of their inferiority complex. If a group is coming out with two papers, one in Hindi and another in English, the management concentrates more on the English one. This attitude has to change. We have to bring ourselves to such a level that we can tell an English journalist that what I am saying has more factual basis. I am proud of the fact that I say what I have to very forcefully.

Nathmal Sharma
Editor, Deshbandhu

The Press Institute has done a commendable thing in organising this seminar but I hope it doesn't become a fashionable concept like

Gandhiji or environment or transparency. I hope even the term village doesn't become a fashionable term. Whatever we have discussed so far has been about villages but we have not discussed the problems faced by the villagers.

We have been so influenced by politics that everything, including the banner of a newspaper, start with politics. Why is it that the first lead has to do with Laloo or Mayawaṭi or Rabri Devi. The first four columns have to do with the colour of Rabri Devi's saree, colour of the border, what she ate for breakfast and how she scolded her staff while talking to the press or Laloo's eccentricities. And we are talking about rural coverage! We have to correct this trend.

I disagree with the fact that no newspaper has rural reporters or doesn't cover villages or that there are no reporters specialising in rural reporting. There are many papers who do that. *Desh Bandhu* which is published from five places in Madhya Pradesh has its basis in rural reporting it has always been that and it still is.

The Statesman Award for Rural Reporting started by the Calcutta based national daily, was won for the first time by a reporter from *Desh Bandhu*. *Desh Bandhu* won eleven of these awards so for the last five years we have stopped sending entries for it. After all, how many awards can *Desh Bandhu* win for rural reporting?

Desh Bandhu has organised workshops on rural reporting for its correspondents. We also give awards for the best rural reporter. However, after running it for a few years we discontinued it, because all our reporters were the best, there were no second best.

I would like to discuss our network and our approach in villages with a small example. Bilaspur is a tribal belt. It is a big town - there are five ministers from here in the Vidhan Sabha, there is also one deputy CM from this place. In this district is a village Sindurkhar. To reach this you have to cross another tribal village Mandla. Till 1983, no official or politician ever visited this village. After this a Collector went there, there are no connecting roads and even a jeep can get there with difficulty. Under these circumstances, the villagers regarded the visit to be of such historic importance that the baby born on that day was named after the Collector.

During his talks with the villagers he was told that although the village had a school, there was no teacher in it. The Collector then told them that if a teacher from outside is unwilling to come here why don't one of the local lads volunteer to teach?

There was an immediate response and two lads who had failed in the 9th class volunteered and they taught for six months. All these months they were not paid. Ultimately they came to Bilaspur. They came to our paper and also met the Collector. He vaguely remembered the incident so he wrote a letter to the joint director but for a year and a half no action was taken.

We took up the case and wrote persistently about it. Then the Commissioner visited the village and now it is being treated almost like a place of pilgrimage. We had published a story on how the Collector had started the process of education in the village and how there had been no follow-up action. Our persistent reporting on it yielded results and a school has come into being.

I mentioned this incident to emphasise the point that the agriculture related matters are only things that matter. In fact, there has been a bumper harvest and there are even exports. If there is greater awareness among people perhaps there could even be higher production. However, there are other issues that need to be tackled. For instance, there is no drinking water or hundreds of people in the village die of water-borne diseases inevitably after the onset of monsoons. There are hospitals but neither doctors nor medicines. There are schools without teachers. The *Desh Bandhu* team was the first to reach this village.

As per the figures about Rs. 400 crores has been spent in the villages in the last six years. I am sorry to say that this amount is being spent purposelessly. For instance, in our village we make *jayat khamb* in memory of our guru. We pray on these. There are thousands of these in the village now. When our representatives went to the village they donated money depending on the requirements of making these *khambs.* What was the use? What is the productivity of these? This is a small example to show where the government has spent Rs. 400 crores.

Likewise there are other ways in which it has been spent. If it had not been spent like this villages would have had roads and electricity and water. The situation is similar to what is happening in the larger villages as well. There was a firing in the home minister's hometown 13 years ago because there was no water there. In a people's agitation for water, there was firing and a boy, a lone child, was killed in that firing. We published the report. But let me inform you that the town still has a water problem.

I would again like to repeat that the priority given to news in a paper needs very serious rethinking. I would have been satisfied if the banners had been on scientific thought and scientific discoveries. Despite the progress made by the electronic media, the print media is still important. People read newspapers because of the credibility and the reality that it provides to a news item. In such a scenario, the priorities of the papers have to change. The actual situation should be written about. Therefore, we need to revise our priorities.

Ruchir Garg
Chief Reporter, Desh Bandhu, Raipur

We have been talking about rural reporting but I think we even need to focus on a rural reporter. We need to discuss the conditions under which a reporter works in a village. It is a big problem which has to be brought on the agenda at the national level. Let me give you an example. Pati Ram Jaiswal is one of our correspondents in Dhantari, a tehsil headquarters. He has been transferred not because he is dishonest but because he is very honest. It is 20 years now since he has been working. He still lives in poverty. A minister has filed a report of stealing against him. He had been accused of 60-65 crimes by the minister. This is a very small instance of repression against a reporter.

In a zila of Bastar, Mohan Rathore, the mafia, politicians and the police got together and he was murdered in broad daylight. Not a single person was willing to go to court. We sent two teams of journalists from Raipur who have submitted reports, but the MP government took a month to figure out that he was not a yellow journalist. He was accused of being a yellow journalist because he had a jeep. The logic was that he could not afford a jeep on his salary so he must be indulging in some underhand work. The point is that after our teams went it took the Chief Minister a month to realise that he had taken a loan for the jeep. After this, we do not know whether he was convinced, but Rs. 1 lakh was given to his family.

The entire village knows why he was murdered. It is being accepted that every journalist in a village is a 'yellow' journalist and we are having a problem dealing with this. I think those in Delhi need to bring this on the agenda. Is a journalist expected to run his house and also work with the Rs. 250 that he gets every month for stationery? We need to focus attention on this.

While the one thing that is worrying is all that we are publishing about villages, is it being read by villagers? If we have to get more villagers to read what we are writing, we need to include terms from the language they use.

Following up news is as important as reporting on the genesis of the news. If what a newspaper is writing is worth following up then the other papers should follow it up both at the regional and national levels. This cooperation should exist at all levels from correspondents to publishers.

Upendra Vajpayee
Secretary General, National Media Centre

I will recapitulate the points that have been discussed in the last two days. First, we start on the assumption that we are a very powerful group which believes that we will be able to deliver more to more people than we have been able to. We are seeking to empower the people in the country who have remained powerless after independence. Newspapers have not been able to discharge their duties properly and this thought has brought us together. In a way we are drawing our own attention to realities before us. A corrolary to empowering people is that we do not have to become power brokers ourselves. The nexus between the press and politicians will always be in danger and we have to guard ourselves against this.

We talk about rural reporting because people in villages have the same rights as those in the cities. The government has failed, the administration and, by and large, even newspapers have failed. They have not been able to attend to the neglected areas, which cover 70 per cent of the total area of the country. This has aggravated social and information imbalances in the country. The invisible danger that if this disparity continues forever, society will not tolerate it and as newspapers we have a duty to ensure that there is some semblence of equity when it comes to providing information to these areas.

The language of the Hindi press has also changed. The role of Hindi is becoming narrow and we have to break out of these narrow confines. We have to include one word from the area where we go because language is the most potent instrument for conveying what we want.

Our independence is being curbed by the government and the links the proprietors have with politicians, there is also the mafia and the terrorist groups.

A relationship has to be drawn between what are the rights of the people and what the ground realities are. This will lead to more involvement by readers from different parts of the country to say starvation deaths in one village. For this I think legal consciousness is very essential as it brings about a basic consciousness of the rights of the people.

Ajit Bhattacharjea

We should be realistic in evolving our views. Realistic in the sense that how ever much we realise the need for rural reporting and social reporting, it cannot ever compete with hard news reporting. The editor always has a difficult job of balancing these conflicting claims on space. In every case, the editor is not willfully doing something which the others may not like, but he has to keep his reader in mind. He has to sell his paper. If he is unable to sell his paper, the best of coverage is wasted. He can sell his paper if it has certain ingredients which have been found, in this country and elsewhere in the world, to be saleable. And those as you all know are crime, sex and in our country political personalities more than anything else. I think some papers have tried to play down this aspect of news and have gone out of business. So this is a fact of life which we in this business must face.

What do we do then because there is some space left? We use it for the kind of coverage we are talking about. But this kind of coverage to merit that space and to compete with hard news must be very well written, must get across to the reader and must sound authentic. It should not sound like a lecture or a handout. That is why this kind of coverage is more difficult than any other kind.

That is why we have been laying so much of emphasis on technique. It is really technique that gets this kind of coverage across. As you have seen from various experiences of the speakers. That is realism from one side. The other realism has to do with what is a correspondent expected to do? We cannot expect him to write literature. There are limitations to his time, and also limitations to his access to information. Therefore, the need is for training. But we should not expect too much.